David W...
(1971, winner...
Standard Award for Most...
Melbourne Critics Eric Award, Australian Writers Guild AWGIE Award for Best Australian Stage Play *and* for Best Script in Any Medium, GLUGGS Award for Contribution to Australian Theatre, Henry Lawson Grenfell Award), *Don's Party* (1971, winner of the Australian Writers Guild AWGIE Award for Best Australian Stage Play), *The Department* (1974, winner of the National Professional Theatre Award), *The Club* (1977, winner of the National Professional Theatre Award and Australian Writers Guild AWGIE Award for Best Stage Play), *Travelling North* (1979, winner of the Australian Writers Guild AWGIE Award for Best Australian Stage Play), *Emerald City* (1987, Sydney Theatre Critics Award for Best Play), *Brilliant Lies* (1993, Special Award for both the play and the film, United Nations Association of Australia Media Peace Awards), and *Soulmates* (2002).

David Williamson's award-winning screenplays include *Don's Party* (1976), *Gallipoli* (1981), *The Year of Living Dangerously* (1981), *Phar Lap* (1982) and *The Perfectionist* (1986). He has also written many acclaimed plays and series for television and radio.

DAVID WILLIAMSON

Up for Grabs

faber and faber

First published in Australia in 2001 by Currency Press Pty Ltd
PO Box 2287, Strawberry Hills, NSW 2012, Australia
First published in this version 2002 by Faber and Faber Limited
3 Queen Square London WC1N 3AU
Published in the United States by Faber and Faber Inc.
an affiliate of Farrar, Straus and Giroux LLC, New York

Typeset by Country Setting, Kingsdown, Kent CT14 8ES
Printed in England by Mackays of Chatham plc, Chatham, Kent

A CIP record for this book is available
from the British Library

0-571-21702-8

2 4 6 8 10 9 7 5 3 1

Up for Grabs received its world première by the Sydney
Theatre Company at the Drama Theatre, Sydney Opera
House, on 1 March 2001, with the following cast:

Simone Helen Dallimore
Gerry Simon Burke
Mindy Kirstie Hutton
Kel Felix Williamson
Dawn Tina Bursill
Felicity Angela Punch McGregor
Manny Garry McDonald

Directed by Gale Edwards
Set Design Brian Thomson
Costume Design Jennifer Irwin
Lighting Design John Rayment
Musical Supervisor Max Lambert

The setting for this version of the play is Sydney.

Up For Grabs was produced by Sonia Friedman for
Sonia Friedman Productions and Theatre Royal, Bath.
The play was first presented in the UK on 13 May 2002
at Wyndham's Theatre, London, with the following cast
(in alphabetical order):

Mindy Megan Dodds
Gerry Tom Irwin
Manny Davis Michael Lerner
Loren Madonna
Kel Daniel Pino
Dawn Grey Sian Thomas
Phyllis Davis Debora Weston

Directed by Laurence Boswell
Set Design Jeremy Herbert
Costume Design Arianne Phillips
Lighting Design Mark Henderson
Sound Design Fergus O'Hare for Aura
Projection Jon Driscoll and Richard Overall
Music Simon Bass

The setting for this version of the play is New York.

Characters

Loren

Gerry

Kel

Mindy

Dawn Grey

Manny Davis

Phyllis Davis

UP FOR GRABS

Act One

SCENE ONE

The Met. New York. Day.
 A slim woman, Loren, dressed in a manner that declares she has expensive and innovatively fashionable taste, walks to the front of the stage and looks up at something above her eyeline.

Loren (*to audience*) Marcel Duchamp said that art dealers were lice on the back of artists. Being a dealer, it's not an image I find appealing or accurate. I think religion provides a much better metaphor. If the artist is God, gripped in the epiphany of divine creation, then we are the priests, interpreting, explaining, and giving insights into God's all too frequently mysterious handiwork. To whom do we give these insights? To the only congregation that matters in the high church of Art. The wealthy. Preferably the obscenely wealthy. My feelings towards the wealthy are deeply ambivalent. On one hand I hate them with a passion. They're a constant reminder that I haven't succeeded. Yet. On the other hand I love them because they are the only ones who can make *me* wealthy Don't get me wrong. I'm not a crass materialist. I want money so I can own beauty.
 Something like that. (*She looks up at a painting.*) For most collectors, art is purely commerce. If I owned a painting like that, there's no way I'd ever sell it. If we're stranded half way between ape and angel – that – (*She looks up at the painting again.*) – is angel.

SCENE TWO

Loren and Gerry's apartment. Upper West Side. Day.
Gerry walks onstage, furious.

Gerry (*waving a credit card statement*) What's this?

Loren What?

He shoves the credit card statement under her nose.

Gerry Lunches three days in a row at Balthazar? Where two shrimps cost twenty-five bucks. And what kind of dress costs twenty-five hundred dollars?! Loren, will you face reality? I can't afford the lifestyle you're living. The Sultan of Brunei could barely afford the lifestyle you're living.

Loren Gerry, I'm working my butt off.

Gerry You're running around spending *my* money.

Loren Big money buys big art. You take big money out, you pay.

Gerry The trickle-*up* theory of economics?

Loren It's an investment, Gerry.

Gerry Honey, an investment is this thing that you do that gets you *returns*.

Loren And we'll get them. Just have faith.

Gerry (*waving the credit card statement*) Faith's not going to help when the guy from Visa arrives to break my legs. Twenty-five hundred dollars for a dress?

Loren What do you think? I'm going to sell art wearing jeans and a T-shirt?

Gerry Who the fuck are you lunching with at Balthazar?

Loren Collectors, Gerry.

Gerry So have they bought anything?

Loren Not exactly, but . . .

Gerry Isn't that what collectors are supposed to do? Did they buy anything?

Loren I told you I wasn't going to become the most successful dealer in town overnight.

Gerry You didn't tell me your two biggest investors were going to be me and the bank! You've made one deal in three years. Three years! Or have I missed some?

Loren Gerry. I went to the Met. today –

Gerry You'll do a lot of business there!

Loren Will you listen to me?

Gerry Tell me why the fuck I should. Our savings are totally blown and I'm about to have to sell the apartment to clear our debt. I mean look at this view. An apartment like this was my dream.

Loren Can I please –

Gerry I've done poor. I don't want to revisit.

Loren Will you just –

Gerry My folks are *still* pinching pennies. A meal out once a month. It's not a life, Loren.

Loren Gerry, I've got a plan.

Gerry For three years you *haven't* had a plan?

Loren The paintings I'm selling are second-rate.

Gerry Now she tells me.

Loren And I can't get my hands on the big stuff until I make a name for myself, so –

Gerry I'm not going to lose this apartment. And I'm not going any further into debt. Not for you, not for anyone. Please, Loren, go back into marketing.

Loren Selling genius excites me. Increasing the market share of Cheesits in Minneapolis does not.

Gerry That would make sense to me if you *were* selling genius. But you're not.

Loren Listen to me, OK? I went to the Met.

Gerry Yeah, yeah. So what?

Loren Occasionally I like to remember the little kid who stood there totally blown away by what she saw.

Gerry Yeah, by the light in a Vermeer. I've heard all this.

Loren Gerry!

Gerry And how you were freaked out by Leonardo's brush-strokes and how your mother had to drag you out of there.

Loren Will you listen to me? I stood there looking at those masterpieces and suddenly I thought, 'Oh My God, that's the way to go.'

Gerry And walked out with Vermeer under your coat?

Loren Are you finished?

Gerry I will be if you keep spending my money.

Loren Listen! David Truscott has the last great privately owned Pollock and I heard a whisper today at Balthazar. His marriage is in deep shit.

Gerry So?

Loren So, I sell him the idea of a quick private sale and he can hide the cash before the property split.

Gerry Will he go for that?

Loren Duh? I'll find three stooges who need a social boost – that shouldn't be very hard – and I'll start a bidding war and get him a price way above market value.

Gerry Is all this ethical?

Loren No. That's why it'll work.

Gerry So what's the Pollock worth?

Loren At least eighteen million. Work out the commission on that.

Gerry Shit.

Loren Do you want kids, Gerry?

Gerry If we don't do it soon I'll be rolling up to their High School graduation in a wheelchair!

Loren They're expensive.

Gerry Ten per cent of eighteen million is . . .

Loren . . . is one point eight million.

Gerry Wow.

Loren Don't give up on me, Grandpa. I'm so close.

She holds up two fingers with a tiny gap between them. Gerry thinks it over.

Gerry Alright. You get two weeks. That's all.

Loren Two weeks?

Gerry Two weeks! Then it's back into marketing and earn money like the rest of us.

Loren Gerry, that's not enough time.

Gerry Two weeks. Then I take a pair of scissors to every credit card you own. (*Gerry moves off.*)

Loren (*to audience*) Terror focuses the mind. And thank God, Truscott bought the scheme and I found my stooges. I invited them to David's apartment to view the Pollock –

SCENE THREE

David Truscott's apartment. Afternoon.
  Kel and Mindy appear.

Loren (*to audience*) – Kel and Mindy. They run a high-speed gift and flower delivery website for people whose relationships are about to disintegrate called Damage Control dot com. (*She turns to Kel, pointing upwards to the Pollock.*)

Loren Well, there it is.

Mindy It's beautiful.

Loren Now that is one of the finest Jackson Pollocks.

Kel You want my honest opinion? It's dated.

Loren (*to audience*) Dated? One of contemporary art's great *masters*?

Kel It's so last century.

Loren (*to audience*) What's he want? A painting that's just dried? (*to Kel*) You think it's *dated*?

Kel Pollock and the abstract expressionists had their moment in time, but art's moved on.

Mindy So how come he's got so many websites?

Kel Sweetie. He's still iconic. Sex, booze, drugs. Died tragically just before he became a total bore. Yeah, all that shit.

Loren I think you'll find that his current prices –

Kel I'm here for his future prices and, standing here looking at that, I'm worried. How long will the icon shit last?

Loren (*to audience*) Longer than you'll be around, moron. (*to Mindy*) I think he's the safest investment there is. In five years' time the price will have doubled.

Kel So why would a smart operator like Truscott be selling?

Loren The big D.

Mindy Divorce.

Loren He doesn't want his wife to grab it.

Mindy Convert assets to cash then hide the cash?

Loren Precisely.

Kel (*to Mindy, suspiciously*) You planning something?

Mindy (*shakes head vigorously*) I saw a guy try it on – *Ally McBeal*.

Loren (*simultaneously*) *Ally McBeal*.

Mindy Kel, I love the painting, can we offer?

Loren Kel? She loves the painting.

Kel What does Truscott want for it?

Loren He won't name a price. He just wants offers.

Kel Offers? Is someone else after this?

Loren Well, yeah. He said, 'I have at least two other competing buyers.'

Kel Hold on, hold on, time out. You said we could buy it. Now it's an *auction*?

Loren No, no. All you need to do is get a sealed envelope to me next Tuesday with your offer.

Mindy And that's it. Highest wins?

Loren No, then you get a chance to top the highest offer.

Kel That's a fucking auction!

Loren No, no. Well, in a minor sort of sense, I guess it is. (*She shrugs helplessly.*) Sorry. That's David Truscott.

Kel Who are the other two buyers?

Loren They prefer to remain anonymous, OK?

Kel So how do we know their offers are real?

Loren I'm not going to blow this deal by letting top offer go to a fake bid.

Kel No, sorry. Auctions are emotion traps. If you ever allow emotion to pollute your decisions, you're dead.

Mindy So how did you pick me? Price-to-earnings ratio?

Kel Business decisions. Baby, c'mon. (*to Loren, looking at the picture*) Sorry, it's not talking to me. It's not talking future. It's not talking capital gains.

Mindy Kel, we're not here for fucking capital gains. We're here to buy beauty.

Kel Beauty? Hello! Mindy, since when have you been an expert on beauty?

Mindy Kel –

Kel That eyeball-busting yellow convertible you bought. Three days later you won't fucking drive it!

Mindy It didn't look so bright in the goddam showroom!

Kel You think I'm going to risk millions and millions of dollars on *your* sense of beauty?

Mindy Put me down as usual, but I'll tell you something. That painting *is* talking to me and it's saying, 'I will enrich your lives.' And I'm listening. So how about you start listening too! 'Bye, Loren. (*She storms off.*)

Loren I guess you two still have a few things to sort out. Here's my card.

Kel takes the card and fidgets off the stage.

(*to audience*) She wants it, he doesn't. What are my chances? Good. A recent survey of 1600 male-female relationships showed that the ones that survived were the ones where the men did what they were told.

SCENE FOUR

David Truscott's place. Next day.
A forty-year-old woman, Dawn, extremely well dressed, but a little too severe to be called attractive, walks towards Loren.

Loren Dr Grey. Good to meet you in person.

Dawn Dawn. Please call me Dawn.

Loren There it is.

Dawn smiles distantly, nods, and looks at the picture.

Loren (*to audience*) Dawn Grey. Grey Dawn. Do people grow more like their names? I can't read this one. In a profession that needs to be able to read people, Dawn Grey is scary.

Dawn (*to audience*) I hate it. Pollock was one of those brutishly macho post-war poseurs who led a blatantly self-destructive, attention-grabbing life, hoping the gullible would confuse the artist with his art. But then again that's just an opinion, and probably not even my own. The more education you have, the more you realise that your so-called 'knowledge' is little more than a huge mental junk box full of other people's conflicting opinions. Then you're sent out into a world where the only saleable commodity is certainty. The last thing people want from an 'expert' is doubts. How do I cope? Look wise and say nothing.

Loren (*to Dawn*) I love it. I think it's one of his very best. But then I don't have a PhD in fine arts, do I?

Dawn No.

Loren Have you enjoyed the shift out of curating and into the corporate sector?

Dawn I'm not in the corporate sector. I'm a consultant.

Loren So how's that –?

Dawn It's been a challenge.

Loren (*to audience*) Over-educated bitch.

Dawn (*to audience*) 'Get us a blue chip signature,' my corporate bosses said. 'A Pollock.' 'Absolutely,' I said. Some consultant.

Dawn Is there a reserve?

Loren Yes.

Dawn I hope David hasn't set an unrealistically high figure.

Loren He wants a good price.

Dawn He would.

Loren You know him?

Dawn I advised him for the while. My clients don't want this to drag on.

Loren Well, I'd like to have this sorted out by next Tuesday night.

Dawn Fine. Call me to confirm a time.

Loren And these days Pollock is taking the same kind of money as Picasso, but I don't need to tell you that, do I?

Dawn No.

Loren (*to audience*) This is not a woman I'd ever want to play poker with. (*to Dawn*) I'll be in touch.

Dawn Thank you.

Loren Thank you.

> *Dawn turns to go.*

(*to audience, feigning shivering*) Anyone feel a draught in here?

> *Loren refocuses her attention on the Pollock. Dawn, behind her, watches her looking at the painting.*

Dawn (*to audience, indicating Loren*) I think she actually *does* like the Pollock. When I was a child, I used to dream that one day I'd paint paintings that people looked at like that. Reverence. That's what I wanted. Reverence for a talent I didn't – unfortunately – turn out to have. (*She leaves the stage.*)

David Truscott's place. Late afternoon.
  Loren leads back Manny and Phyllis Davis towards the painting.

Loren Mr and Mrs Davis. Thank you for coming.

Manny What's this Phyllis tells me about an auction?

Loren I explained to Mrs Davis that it's the only way David will sell.

Manny So where is he? Hiding in the back?

Loren He's in Georgia playing golf.

Manny He knows I'm one of the prospective buyers, doesn't he?

Loren No, he doesn't.

Manny Yes, he does.

Loren I swear he doesn't.

Manny Excuse me . . .? What do you call yourself?

Loren Loren.

Manny Loren, If he finds out I'm one of the buyers he'll put the price up.

Loren He doesn't know it's you and I won't be telling him.

Phyllis Loren, I am so glad you rang. I've wanted a major Pollock for years.

Manny Laid a canvas on the floor and dripped paint on it. Where's the art in that?

Phyllis It's a living record of his life energy and state of mind when he did it.

Manny You know what *Time* magazine called him? Jack the Dripper.

Phyllis Manny, this is the *only* great Pollock still held privately.

Manny That's brilliant, Phyllis. Why don't you get a megaphone and announce to David Truscott – (*He indicates Loren.*) – that you have to have his painting and will pay whatever it takes?

Phyllis Manny, I have waited years for a quality Pollock! I've been ashamed for years at the dross that's hanging on our walls, and –

Manny Dross! Four Raushenbergs, five Warhols, three de Koonings, a Rothko –

Phyllis A minor Rothko, three totally forgettable de Koonings and not *one* Pollock. And to anyone who knows anything Pollock is the big hitter.

Manny Two Jasper John's. No, three.

Phyllis And *no* Pollocks.

Manny An Ashile Gorky

Phyllis And *no* Pollocks.

Manny Because you can't get 'em!

Phyllis Because you wouldn't pay when one came up! You keep telling me you're the twelfth richest man in New York City, well for Christ's sake you wouldn't know it looking at what's on our walls.

Manny (*to Phyllis*) Look, I'm here to get this painting – would you shut the fuck up? – I'm not letting David Truscott screw me!

Phyllis You think *everyone* tries to screw you.

Manny David Truscott is a greedy, dishonest, pretentious snob –

Phyllis You play golf with him.

Manny Kicks his ball into better lies. Thinks I don't see.

Phyllis Then why *keep* playing golf with him?

Manny Because I win. And he keeps playing because he's determined to beat me. Gets lessons. Secretly.

Phyllis So do you.

Manny He started it. Look, you want this painting, fine, but I won't be robbed. (*to Loren*) What's the ballpark figure?

Loren Eighteen million.

Manny For random dribbles?

Phyllis Manny!

Loren In five years' time it'll be worth double.

Manny It's too much. Seventeen million is all it's worth. I've checked.

Phyllis (*warning*) Manny . . .

Manny No one's ever screwed Manny Davis, and David Truscott's not going to be the first.

> *Manny looks at Phyllis belligerently, turns and goes. Phyllis glares after him, gives a stiff smile.*

Phyllis He'll buy it. He owes me. But he'll only pay what it's worth. Tell David we want his painting, but we're not fools.

Loren I understand.

Phyllis I want that painting. And if I get it at the right price I'll do business with you again.

Loren I understand.

Phyllis I've been looking for someone I can trust.

Phyllis nods and moves off. Loren watches her go.

Loren (*to audience*) Two pairs of real buyers and one possible. Not bad. My optimism, however, was short-lived.

SCENE SIX

Loren's apartment. Later that evening.
  Loren moves and sits down.

Loren (*to audience*). People who collect art are usually weird, but at least I can take their money and run. Gerry is stuck with weirdos eight hours a day. He's a therapist.

Gerry Depressives! (*imitating one*) 'I'm useless, I'm hopeless, I'm worthless.' After fifty minutes of that you're itching to say, 'You're right.'

Loren Hi, Gerry –

Gerry Neurotics irritate the hell out of me. Terrified of every little step they take – (*He stretches his feet out tentatively as he acts out someone threading their way through a minefield.*) – but at least they keep walking. But depressives . . . (*He shakes his head in horror.*)

Loren We have to talk.

Gerry Even *paranoids* are better than depressives. Dangerous, but at least they don't whine. (*He sighs.*) How's the Pollock auction coming along?

*Loren says nothing but Gerry's in full flight and
doesn't notice.*

You know, the chilling thing is that last year there was
a big study published in the *Journal of Psychotherapy*,
comparing how people assessed their talent with their
real level of talent, and the only group that didn't grossly
overestimate themselves were depressives.

Loren still says nothing.

Don't you think that's chilling? It means the only way we
get through life is deluding ourselves that we're a lot
smarter and more creative than we actually are. We
believe our own bullshit, and if we believe, we convince
others. Depressives are the only ones who see themselves
honestly and so they never get anywhere and get even
more depressed. Frightening, huh? (*He looks at Loren's
face for the first time.*) So what's wrong with you?

Loren is silent.

You said it was all systems go.

Loren is silent. Gerry starts to panic.

What – tell me!

Loren David Truscott took his Pollock off the market.

Gerry But he gave you his word.

Loren He found out Manny Davis was one of the buyers
(*imitating David Truscott*) You want it – it's mine – fuck
off!

Gerry The deepest levels of hate I've ever experienced in
therapy are between golf partners. The deal's off?

Loren No, I got on the phone to repair the damage.

Gerry And?

Loren And David finally said OK, I'll sell, but only if I get enough to compensate for the fact that that prick Manny might get it.

Gerry So what's he want for it?

Loren Twenty million.

Gerry He won't get twenty.

Loren Why not? 'Lavender Mist' was valued at well over forty.

Gerry 'Lavender Mist' is the big one.

Loren I'm selling an important painting, Gerry.

Gerry If he's put a reserve of twenty on it, it won't sell.

Loren Gerry, I had to make a snap decision.

Gerry (*growing horror*) What the fuck have you done?

   Loren looks away.

Loren I've *guaranteed* him the twenty.

Gerry (*shakes his head in disbelief*) No. No!

Loren He gave me an hour to fax back the agreement, or the deal was off.

Gerry You've totally lost it.

Loren I'm sure I can get them there.

Gerry Loren!

Loren If I get them up to twenty-one we make a million dollars. I had to take the risk.

Gerry You've committed us to a potential debt of two million dollars.

Loren Sometimes life goes nowhere unless you close your eyes and jump.

Gerry When your partner is tied to your goddam ankles, maybe you ask him first!

Loren Gerry, I am deeply ashamed that you've been the breadwinner all these years. It's a situation I swore I'd never ever get myself into. This is my chance to earn self-respect.

Gerry Honey, this just isn't fair!

Loren I *can* get them up over twenty. I know I can.

Gerry I can't believe you've done this. I can't believe it.

Loren I shouldn't have. I know. I know you're not a risk-taker by nature.

Gerry What?

Loren I knew you'd be angry, but –

Gerry I want to be consulted before my life is ruined, so I'm not a risk-taker?

Loren I'm not blaming you. I know your father was the same.

Gerry You think I'm like my *father*?

Loren No, but –

Gerry I *hate* the way my father lives. The neatness, the sterility, the clipped hedges – you think that's me?

Loren No, of course not, but –

Gerry My parents are both pathological obsessive-compulsives.

Loren I wasn't saying –

Gerry The fact I don't smile in the face of imminent wipeout makes me like my parents?

Loren No, but –

Gerry If there's any parent to blame it's your mother. Recklessness as a way of life.

Loren At least she's not the living dead.

Gerry She has Alzheimer's, and goes on a trekking expedition to the fucking Himalayas.

Loren Mild, she has *mild* Alzheimer's.

Gerry Sure. I pay for the helicopter that finds her, and she gets back and doesn't even remember she's been.

Loren Gerry, I've signed the agreement. There's nothing I can do about it. It's terrifying, but it's also exciting. We don't want to end up at seventy saying, 'If only we'd taken the risk.'

Gerry You know what we'll be saying at seventy? 'Hurry up or we'll be last in line at the soup kitchen.'

    Loren's mobile phone plays Pachabel's 'Canon'.

Loren Loren. Hold on a second.

Gerry Do you know how long it would take us to pay off a debt of two million? Another three lifetimes!

Loren Will you get out of here and let me get on with making this deal work!

Gerry Who is it?

Loren Manny Davis!

Loren Hi, Manny.

Manny Davis's apartment. Upper East Side. Next evening.
    Loren is talking to Manny and Phyllis.

Manny We've changed our minds. We don't want a Pollock, we want a – (*to Phyllis*) – what?

Phyllis A Chagall. He's more . . . spiritual.

Loren Chagall is a great painter, but –

Phyllis I like Pollock, but the more I thought about Chagall and his breathtaking figure–ground contrasts –

Loren (*nodding in agreement*) Absolutely, but the exciting thing about Pollock is that in doing away with the attempt to *depict*, he was the very first to give us painting as *event*. A seismograph recording his spirit and energy at the moment of creation.

Phyllis (*nods*) Yes, that's true, but –

Loren The essence of creativity caught for ever in an instant of time.

Manny What the fuck are you talking about?

Phyllis Don't embarrass me.

Manny We want a Chagall. I know you want to sell us the Pollock because there's more money in it for you, but –

Loren Manny, I'm trying to sell you the Pollock because I don't want you on the phone abusing me in five years when you can't sell your Chagall.

Manny Chagall's never going to drop.

Loren Manny, I'm sorry. Anyone who knows anything knows that Chagall is over.

Manny Bullshit.

Loren Are you buying this painting for your grandmother? As I understood it, Manny, you were chasing capital gains and Phyllis, you were looking for a 'Wow' painting.

Phyllis Certainly something that would be . . . noticed.

Loren Chagall is nice. Bourgeois-decorative nice. But the kind of painting that blows people away . . . Well, I'm sorry. That's not Chagall.

Phyllis There's no doubt Pollock is more . . .

Manny Expensive?

Phyllis . . . dramatic.

Loren Look, I appreciate Chagall's spiritual qualities myself, but if we're talking raw power, if we're talking 'Wow' factor, then –

Phyllis (*nods*) It's Pollock.

Loren (*to Manny*) And Pollock's intrinsic value, Manny, is going up and up.

Manny Then why would a smartass like Truscott be selling?

Loren (*to Phyllis*) What scares a rich man most?

   Phyllis knows instantly.

Phyllis A 'D & P S'?

Manny What?

Phyllis A divorce and property split.

Loren (*nods*) He gave his girlfriend a BMW convertible and his wife found out.

Manny The game-show bimbo?

Loren Bingo!

Manny (*gleeful*) There is a God. There *is* a God.

Phyllis (*to Manny*) How do you know about her?

Manny No use having a bimbo unless you can brag about it.

Phyllis Listen, mister – You better not be buying convertibles for any bimbos.

Manny Sweetheart. I know what David doesn't. Lose control of your dick, you lose control of your assets. I don't do that stuff.

Loren (*to audience*) Which is true. With Manny you hear ruthless, treacherous, cunning, but never bimbos. Which is odd.

Manny (*to Loren, still elated at David's downfall*) Probably David's wife would've been OK with a standard BMW but a convertible was over her pain threshold.

Phyllis (*to Manny*) Don't you ever try anything. My pain threshold is extremely low.

Manny Don't I know it.

Phyllis I mean it.

Manny I've suffered enough at your hands already. You think I'd give you an excuse to impoverish me? Now do you want the Pollock or the Russian guy?

Phyllis The Pollock.

Manny As if I didn't know. In our whole life have you ever taken the cheaper option?

24

Phyllis There has to be *some* upside to living with you.

Loren Manny, send me an envelope with your offer before next Tuesday and you might just end up with the art buy of the century.

Manny looks her up and down.

Manny No envelopes.

Phyllis Manny.

Manny looks at Loren again.

Manny No envelopes. Come and see me in my office on Monday at three and I'll tell you what my bid is.

Loren I'd rather have something in writing.

Manny I don't put things like that in writing. Ever. I know exactly what it's worth and that's all I'm going to pay. No more no less. Monday at three.

Loren nods and leaves.

Loren (*to audience*) Phyllis is hooked, but I can't read Manny. Meet me at my office at three?

SCENE EIGHT

Kel and Mindy's apartment. Tribeca. Day.
Kel and Mindy are onstage working furiously on their slimline portable computers as Loren dials on her mobile. Mindy's mobile plays 'Eine Kleine Nachtmusik'. She picks up her mobile.

Mindy (*into phone*) Mindy McEwen. Sorry, can you call back?

Dean and Deluccas. Midtown. Day. Intercut.

Loren Mindy, I just need a second.

Mindy Who is it?

Loren Loren.

Mindy Loren who?

Loren We spoke. About the painting?

Mindy Oh yeah. We're sick of the colours in the living room, the bathroom, all the bedrooms and we're after a cost estimate. Can you hang on a second?

Kel Who the fuck's that?

Mindy Office chick from the painting company.

Kel Get her off the line! We're down seventy cents in seven minutes! Shit! That shaves – (*He calculates on a desk calculator.*) – four million off our net worth. In seven minutes! Shit.

Mindy Could you ring back? We're in crisis here.

She hangs up. Mindy and Kel stare trancelike at their screens. Loren gives a hiss of annoyance and wonders whether to ring again.

Kel Steady, we're holding steady. Ah, here we go. We're surging. We're defying market trends. Alone in the IT wreckage, Damage Control dot com is kicking arse again baby. Yow!

Mindy We've picked a winner.

Kel Honey. I picked a winner.

Mindy Kel, there is a hell of a lot of me in this company.

Kel Initial concept. Mine. Sorry, babe. Mine.

Mindy Do you have to let me know all the time?

Kel Ten futurology conferences around the globe, and the only thing *all* of them agreed on was that male–

female relationships were going to go from total disaster to absolutely fucked.

Mindy Does it make you worried?

Kel Worried? Damage Control dot com, relationship-healer extraordinaire, *cannot lose*! Yow!

Mindy About us?

Kel Us? Babe, we've got it all. Relationships break up because of incompatibility of interest, lack of time together, lack of communication. We work together, plan together, eat together, play together –

Mindy Play together? When do we ever play together?

Kel (*raising eyes*) Sunday, babe. Sunday.

He imitates snorting coke and hints at other more carnal pleasures.

Mindy (*flat*) Oh, yeah.

Kel Don't try and tell me you don't have fun.

Mindy Yeah, but like . . . picnics.

Kel Picnics? You want to do stuff out in the open air?

Mindy *Real* picnics. Some French bread, fancy cheese, bottle of wine. Looking at stuff. Y'know, mountains and brooks.

Kel Yeah? Brooks?

Mindy Bubbling brooks. Over stones.

Kel OK. Sure. I'll check it out. (*He punches keys on his computer.*) Top ten brooks.

Mindy (*correcting herself*) No, babbling, not bubbling. In that poem. 'I come from haunts of coot and something.'

Kel I'll check it out. (*punching more keys*) Who wrote it?

Mindy No, not babbling. It was 'bickering'.

Kel Bicker? Brooks don't bicker.

Mindy Bicker. It was bicker.

Kel (*shrugs*) OK. (*He punches keys.*). Brook plus bicker plus poetry. Go, Google. Yeah, yeah, yeah. Tennyson. Alfred Lord Tennyson. 'I come from haunts of coot and hern.' What the fuck's a hern? 'I make a sudden sally. And sparkle out among the fern. To bicker down the valley.'

Mindy Isn't that beautiful. Kel, we're losing touch with beauty.

Kel OK, babe. Sunday. I'll find a top brook, get everything pre-delivered. We'll cruise out in the Aston, and then we'll come home and do stuff. Like normal.

Mindy Yeah, well –

Kel If you're getting tired of Gloria . . .

Mindy No, it's . . . Gloria's fine.

Kel She is getting a bit fuckin' predictable. And let's face it, she's really letting herself go. Six months ago she was *Playboy* centrefold material. OK. Hey, Gloria and her fat arse are out of here.

Mindy I like her. She's fine. I just don't know whether the whole thing's . . .

Kel Come on. It works for us, honey.

Mindy looks a little dubious.

Gloria. Deleted. (*He punches information into his personal organiser.*) Now let's see who we can find. (*He starts to search the net.*)

Mindy (*flaring*) Kel. Not all the solutions to our problems are on the stupid net.

Kel Honey –

Mindy Our lives have no . . . beauty! No . . . dimension.

Kel Dimension.

Mindy Dimension.

Kel What d'you mean, dimension?

Mindy I don't know what I mean! If I did I'd fucking do something about it.

Kel (*panic-stricken*) Honey. It'll be fine. Whatever the problem is, we'll fix it. Don't say there's a problem. I'm crazy about you. We are the A-team. Look at that screen. We're still surging. You and I, we defy gravity. Dimension. I don't know what you mean.

Mindy No. You don't.

> *Kel stares straight ahead in silent panic. Loren decides it's time to ring again. Mindy's mobile plays 'Für Elise'. She picks it up.*

Loren It's Loren.

Mindy Can you call back?

Loren Can I just have a second?

Mindy Loren? The paint person?

Loren Loren the dealer.

Mindy Oh. Right. Yeah. Got enough for about fifty good lines?

Loren The *art* dealer!

Mindy Art? Oh, shit. The Pollock thing.

Loren That's the one . . .

Mindy (*she puts her hand over the phone*) It's that babe pushing the Pollock. I totally forgot. Could you hold on a second?

Kel Hey, she's it! Forget Gloria. She's it.

Mindy No, Kel.

Kel Get her.

Mindy We shouldn't.

Kel Please.

Mindy (*getting excited*) You're bad, Kel. You're a bad, bad boy! God, she *is* hot. (*She takes her hand off the phone.*) Come over. We'll talk about it.

Loren OK. When?

Mindy Sunday.

Loren What time?

Mindy (*to Kel*) What time?

Kel takes the phone off her.

Kel The sooner the better, honey. It's rest and recreation day. Yow!

Loren How about seven?

Kel You got it. Rock on!

Mindy hangs up.

Mindy Kel, you dork! You'll scare her away!

Kel She wants a deal, honey. (*He winks at her.*) She wants a deal.

Mindy closes her eyes and starts stamping her feet up and down in excitement.

Mindy She is a babe isn't she? She is a *babe*!

Kel And she wants a deal! Stick with me, honey. We're the A-team.

Loren looks at her mobile phone, then frowns, worried.

Loren (*to audience*) I'm back in there with Dork and Mindy, but back for what? Doesn't sound like hot milk and cookies. At least I've still got Dawn, my one rock-solid investor.

SCENE NINE

Loren dials from her apartment.
Dawn's apartment. West Village. Intercut.
Dawn, who is tending her pot plants, answers.

Dawn Dawn Grey.

Loren Dawn, have you got a minute? It's Loren.

Dawn I was about to ring you.

Loren Oh good. It's all going to be decided by ten o'clock Tuesday night. I was just confirming.

Dawn Loren. My clients won't be bidding.

Loren Dawn, not bidding? But your corporation wants a Pollock. And this is Pollock right at his peak. Four paintings later he gave us 'Lavender Mist'.

Dawn I'm sorry for any inconvenience, but circumstances have changed.

Loren Circumstances?

Dawn Yes. Sorry.

Loren Dawn, this is a helluva shock for me. Do you mind if I ask you a few questions?

Dawn I'm not at liberty to discuss company policy.

Loren Is there any other piece of art I could help you with?

Dawn No. I don't think so.

Loren stares into her phone.

Loren Dawn, I've set everything up. Can . . . can you understand I'm a little shocked?

Dawn Of course. I'm sorry.

There's a pause.

It's not really all that confidential any more, I don't suppose. My corporation is merging with a German company and they want to purchase some contemporary German art as a gesture of goodwill.

Loren Dawn, contemporary German art is hideous.

Dawn It can be . . . difficult.

Loren Seriously. Don't you think contemporary German art is hideous?

Dawn (*to audience*) Indeed I do. In the relentless search for heroic grandeur, the German soul has only ever managed grossness. No, that's unfair. It's just another platitude I've picked up from one of the million books I've read on art. I actually have no idea why contemporary German art is so hideous. It just is. (*to Loren*) The thing is, Loren, I haven't seen enough to make a balanced judgement.

Loren I have. And they're going to hate it and blame you. There's another option. Pollock had a German grandmother.

Dawn Sorry. (*Dawn hangs up.*)

Loren (*bitterly*) Thanks a million. (*to audience*) The only thing between me and wipeout? Manny and the dot com vampires. Not a good feeling.

SCENE TEN

Kel and Mindy's loft apartment. Tribeca. Sunday afternoon.
   Kel and Mindy have had quite a few lines of cocaine and they're fidgety as they listen to Loren deliver her spiel.

Loren Who could've picked it. Bimbo gets beamer and the last ever Pollock appears dirt cheap. You want to be serious collectors? This is your dream start.

   Kel and Mindy look at each other and back at Loren.

Mindy You always work Sundays?

Loren Not always, but this is an important painting.

Mindy We made four million cap gains this week.

Loren Wow, that's . . . amazing.

Mindy I don't know how I feel about it. It seems weird.

Kel I know how I feel about it.

   He whoops and snorts another line of coke. Mindy snorts one too. They both look at her. Loren feels uncomfortable and struggles to make conversation.

Loren Really very smart, calling your firm 'Damage Control'. I mean, how many people do you know are in a healthy relationship?

   Kel and Mindy look at her. She plunges nervously on.

Get the name right and the millions flow?

Kel (*shakes head*) No use getting the red roses there *after* she's shot his arse dead. We had to do an intensive crash course in flowers, gifts –

Mindy Marketing –

Kel Management structure, delivery services –

Mindy Accounting, cash-flow management –

Kel Time management, supplier contracts –

Mindy And that was day one. Steep learning curve. Nearly killed us.

Kel It's pure Darwin out there. Two out of a hundred dot coms survive. I had severe heart arrhythmia at the age of twenty-eight.

Mindy That was the coke, Kel.

Kel The coke was so I could keep going.

Mindy It's been hard, believe me.

Loren I do.

Mindy (*offering cocaine*) Hey. You want to do some blow?

Loren No thanks. So?

Mindy The Pollock? I'm not like Kel. I like old things. And hey, we made a lot of money this week so – (*She shrugs.*)

Loren You're going to put in an offer?

Mindy Yeah.

Kel I checked out his prices on the web. Last time a Pollock changed hands, 1989. Twelve million.

Loren You've done your homework.

Kel And here's our offer –

*Kel takes out an envelope and shows it to Loren.
Loren goes to take it, but he whips it behind his back
and chuckles.*

Relax, baby. Chill out.

Loren Maybe I should go.

Mindy No, please. It's Sunday. (*Mindy smiles and gently
pushes Loren back onto a sofa, then moves behind her
and starts to massage her neck.*) Relax.

*Loren finds herself responding to the massage despite
herself.*

Mindy I've been thinking about you a lot.

Loren It's a big decision you've got to make. The
painting.

Mindy continues to massage Loren's neck and back.

Mindy You're so tense. Relax.

Loren I should go.

Kel Hey. *No.*

Mindy (*to Loren*) You work out, right? You have an
amazing body.

Kel nods vigorously in agreement.

You're gorgeous. As if you didn't know.

Loren (*to Mindy*) I really should go.

Mindy kisses her neck.

Mindy You're gorgeous.

Loren I'm married.

Mindy So am I. To him. (*She indicates Kel.*)

Mindy You've never . . . with women?

Loren I've dabbled.

Mindy kisses her on the lips. Loren allows it to happen for a while then pulls away.

Mindy You're not sure about this, are you?

Loren No.

Mindy Is it because he's watching?

Loren It doesn't help.

Mindy turns to Kel.

Mindy Can I tell her? Why we do this stuff?

Kel, with the suspicion of a tear in his eye, nods.

Before Damage Control dot com, we were just a pair of struggling IT kids. But the minute we saw each other we clicked. Except Kel had this obsession.

Kel I wanted to be bigger.

Mindy He had this operation. They pull it out from the inside and take fat from the thighs and stuff it like they're stuffing a bratwurst sausage. Now he's got the biggest dick you've ever seen. Awesome.

Kel nods.

Kel Fucking huge.

Mindy But they blew it. It bends up like a hoop.

Kel nods mournfully.

He sued the surgeon and we got a small fortune, which we've now turned into a large fortune, but hey, it really takes the gloss off being rich when the man you love has a dick like a giant doughnut.

Kel You provoked me –

Mindy Kel –

Kel Every time we'd do a line or two and watch a porno, you'd go 'Wow', and I'd say, 'It's not *that* much bigger than mine,' and silence. *Total* silence!

Mindy You can admire the extraordinary without having to have it!

Kel I *wanted* you to have it! (*Kel stares ahead, tearfully.*)

Mindy (*to Loren*) So all he can do now –

Kel – is watch.

   Mindy looks at Loren. Mindy nods.

Mindy If this kind of stuff freaks you, just say.

Loren I've got a husband.

Mindy He can watch too.

   Kel holds out his mobile phone.

Loren I don't think it's his sort of thing.

   Mindy smiles and continues stroking Loren.

Mindy The social conditioning thing is hard to shake, so if this is freaking you . . .

Loren (*to audience*) Freaking me? Believe me I am not into this sort of thing. I hate porn, and my 'dabbling' consisted of kissing a few girlfriends when I was fourteen, but I feel like I'm in one of those dreams where your body refuses to take orders from your brain.

Mindy If it's feeling good, don't feel guilty. Science has proved that absolutely *everyone* is potentially bi.

   Loren's body continues to refuse to take orders from her brain.

Kel and Mindy's apartment. Some time later.

Loren (*to audience, adjusting her dress*) Letting myself be seduced by a woman was one thing, but letting it all happen while there was a man nearby grasping something that looked like a huge misshapen cucumber was . . . strange. I told myself that I'd only done it because I was a ruthless dealer baiting the hook, but if that was the case, how come I enjoyed it? I told myself I'd been manipulated by a pair of ruthless kinks who'd dangled the bait of their bidding power in order to use me for their perverted gratification. And then I told myself – they'll pay. Big time. More than twenty million dollars.

Kel and Mindy enter.

(*taking it*) I'll call you Tuesday at seven and let you know how your offer stands.

Mindy I hope we didn't –

Loren No, no. No.

Kel hands Loren the envelope.
Seconds later: Loren opens the envelope and reads.

Sixteen point five. Hopeless. I'm still three point five million short. But at least it's an offer.

Her mobile plays Vivaldi's 'Four Seasons – Winter'.

Manny Davis. Shit. He's going to cancel the appointment. (*to the audience, seconds later*) He didn't cancel. He changed the venue. He wants me to meet him in his permanent suite in his favourite hotel. The place where he gets away to think, he said.

Manny's penthouse hotel room. Afternoon.
  Loren walks in. Manny's there, sitting on a sofa,
waiting for her.

Loren Manny, the guy at reception looked at me like
I was a hooker.

Manny You *are* a hooker, aren't you? You're trying to
sell me something for more than it's worth and you'll do
anything to get your price.

Loren Oh yeah? Try me.

Manny You think I've brought you here to screw you?

Loren It's crossed my mind.

Manny This is where I do all my strategic thinking. You
think I've got all these computers hooked up here so
I can screw people? Please – (*He indicates for her to sit.*)
The painting. It's worth seventeen tops. No more.

Loren I've already got an offer way above that.

Manny But nowhere near the minimum that you
guaranteed David right?

Loren I haven't given him a guarantee.

Manny Bullshit. The story's all round town. Got you
desperate and made you sign. Twenty million, right?

  Loren looks worried. She says nothing.

You're about to lose a fortune.

Loren (*brave face*) Wrong. I've got a very strong offer
already.

Manny Of what?

39

Loren Are you going to put in a *real* offer, Manny? Seventeen is laughable.

Manny You're a clever operator, Loren. You made my wife desperate for a 'Wow' painting, and if I don't get it my life will be hell. But you know something, the *ultimate* hell would be to see David Truscott gloating over the fact that I'd paid him more than it was worth. (*He looks at her.*) Seventeen. And that, honey, is all you're going to get. (*He leans back and surveys her.*) You're in big trouble, aren't you?

Loren lowers her head, trying desperately to stop the tears flowing.

Loren I'm not going to fuck you, Manny.

Manny I don't want you to.

Loren You want me to do something.

Manny Yeah, sure I do. Have done from the moment I set eyes on you, but it's not going to happen.

Loren looks at Manny.

Loren (*to audience*) I just know this next bit's not going to be pretty. But ask yourself what you'd do if you were staring at a three-million-dollar debt. (*to Manny*) What do you want me to do?

Manny looks at her.

You want me to go down on you? Fine. As long as you offer twenty million, fine.

Manny looks at her.

Come on, Manny. This is what you live for, isn't it? The moment when you get your victim in the glare of the headlights? You want me down on my knees? Let's go. Is that what you want?

Manny No.

Loren Discipline, Manny? You want me to tie you up? That's OK. I can do that. Bring out the handcuffs. I crack a mean whip.

Manny No.

Loren Whatever it is, you can be sure I'm never going to tell anyone.

Manny keeps looking at her.

What is it, Manny? I'm in the headlights. Can't run, can't hide . . .

Manny looks at her and goes to a drawer. He takes out a large latex penis with a harness attached. Loren stares at it.

Oh my God, Manny. That's too big for me.

Manny (*anguished*) It's for me! Eighteen million.

Loren For God's sake, pay a prostitute.

Manny Yeah, and have them on the phone five minutes later selling the information to all my enemies? You've got to be kidding.

Loren No. No way.

Manny Please. Eighteen point five. Come on. You need the money.

Loren stares at him.

Loren No.

Manny I'm begging you, OK. Manny Davis is begging you.

Loren Get a man!

Manny I'm not a *queer*!

Loren You need therapy.

Manny What, and tell some fucking soft cock I want it up the ass!

Loren Manny, you've got problems.

Manny So have you! Nineteen.

Loren No!

Manny Nineteen. That's as high as I'm going to go. (*Holds up the dildo.*) For God's sake. I'm looking at you standing there and going off my fucking brain.

Loren What is this, a joke?

Manny Honey, my life is a joke. No, worse, a lie. I've dutifully fucked my wife for twenty-five years. And it's done nothing for her or me.

Loren You're gay, Manny.

Manny No!

Loren It's not a crime.

Manny I'm not gay! I only want to do this with *women*!

Loren Manny, you're sick!

Manny Don't psychoanalyse me! Just do it. What do you want? You want me on my knees begging?

Loren Twenty million.

Manny Nineteen point five. That's it.

> *Loren takes the harness dildo, looks at it, then waggles it under his chin.*

Loren Twenty.

Manny All right, twenty.

Loren And I want it in writing.

Manny No!

She turns to go.

Manny OK, OK. (*He scribbles something on a piece of paper and hands it to her. She checks it.*)

Loren Here?

Manny Yeah.

Loren Now?

Manny Now. I want to see you naked and I want to see you put it on.

Loren (*to audience*) There are obviously things about the rich you don't find out reading the *Fortune* five hundred. (*She looks at the huge dildo. To audience*) How could I do it? Think two and a half million dollars. It was gross, it was humiliating, but to hear the most detestable human being I've ever met squealing with rapture like a little girl and crying no, no, no, when he really meant yes, yes yes, was strangely empowering. I left with a pledge for twenty million dollars. No profit, no debt.

SCENE THIRTEEN

Loren's apartment. A little later.
Loren walks into her apartment. Gerry looks at her with a mixture of anger and fear.

Gerry Well?

Loren Take the terrified look off your face. It's OK.

Gerry What do you mean?

Loren I've had an offer of twenty million.

Gerry Yes, from who?

Loren Manny Davis.

Gerry Twenty? He knows it's not worth that.

Loren That's what he's offered.

Gerry Manny's smart. Why the hell would he offer twenty?

Loren Because maybe that's what it's worth!

Her mobile plays 'Jesu, Joy of Man's Desiring'. She grabs at it. Dawn is on her mobile phone.

Loren.

Dawn It's Dawn Grey.

Loren Dawn, how are you?

Dawn I'm fine.

Loren Nice to hear from you.

Dawn The merger's fallen through.

Loren whispers this to Gerry.

Loren So . . .?

Dawn I've put in an offer.

Loren An offer? That's wonderful.

Dawn Are you at home?

Loren Yes, yes I am.

Dawn I sent it by courier. You should find it under your door.

Loren Fantastic. I'll get back to you. (*Loren rips open the envelope.*) Eighteen point five. (*She waves the envelope at Gerry. To Gerry*) Not great.

Gerry Yeah, but when she hears that the top offer is twenty, then you really could have an auction on your hands.

Loren And then, Gerry baby, we're going to be filthy rich.

Gerry Balthazar every day, all the shrimps you can eat, six kids –

Loren Easy, tiger.

Gerry And a nanny for every one of them. (*But something's still worrying him.*) Manny offered twenty?

Loren (*defensively*) Yes, he did. Now how about you look me in the eye and tell me I'm not so stupid after all?

Gerry Twenty million dollars?

Loren nods. Gerry looks at her, then starts to nod too. Finally convinced they're in the black.

Loren *and* **Gerry** (*sing*) You sexy mother-fucker!

Loren (*to audience*) I've got an auction. What I'd had to do to get it was something I didn't want to dwell on. I swore I'd never do anything like that again, but then of course, the auction hadn't happened yet.

Act Two

Loren and Gerry's apartment. Tuesday evening.
   Loren is sitting jotting down the arguments she is going to use to try to get the right price. She rehearses one to herself. Gerry looks on.

Loren Honestly, the sky is the limit . . . no, no, *no*! (*She takes a few deep breaths.*) Grandpa, how does this sound? Look, if you want a sure thing, then American Abstract Expressionism's got to be it. People still haven't gotten over the ninety-million-dollar price tag on Van Gogh, but the major players all agree that the man most likely to beat that . . . top that . . . beat that, top that, which is better?

Gerry They're both fine.

Loren Which is better?

Gerry They're both fine!

Loren What's wrong with you? This is money night.

Gerry Yeah. Money night.

Loren It is. You know it is.

Gerry Is it?

Loren I'm hot, look at me. I'm on fire, I've got an auction.

Gerry All you've got is break-even, and even that depends on Manny Davis paying two million more than the painting's worth. OK, we're out of this by the skin of our teeth, but who knows what you're going to risk with the next deal or the next . . . ?

Loren Gerry, you are so negative. Let's see what happens tonight before you start obsessing about the next time and the next time.

Gerry You scared the shit out of me and I'm not going to let it happen again.

Loren What?

Gerry I made sure.

Loren What are you talking about?

Gerry I've talked to my lawyer.

She stares at him.

This is *my* apartment and from now on your debt is your debt.

Loren The apartment's in joint names.

Gerry (*shakes head*) No.

Loren You changed it to joint ownership when we got married. I signed the papers.

Gerry Well, *I* didn't. I had a feeling something like this would happen.

Loren Something like what?

Gerry If I'd been consulted – if we'd sat down and – discussed . . .

Loren What is this? We went out last night. You were happy . . .

Gerry Part of that was sheer fucking relief. Have you any idea of what you put me through these last few days? Thinking I lost all this?

Loren You're telling me it's over between us? That's what you're doing?

47

Gerry Why would you want to hang around me in any case? I'm just Joe Boring. Gerry No-Balls.

Loren Gerry – that was just a joke.

Gerry When anyone tells me I'm like my father, that's no joke. That's vicious.

Loren What is this about? I've got an offer of twenty million. Your precious apartment is perfectly safe.

Gerry You made me feel like a *total* fucking wimp, you humiliated me and I woke up in the middle of last night and said, 'Fuck this, why should I live my life in acute terror?' I'm sorry. Find some other adrenaline junkie to share your life with. I'm happy with my life the way it is. (*He turns to go.*)

Loren This is just what I need two minutes before the biggest play of my life. Thank you, Gerry.

Gerry Don't self-dramatise. You're a borderline hysteric.

Loren I have had to work like you wouldn't believe to get this happening.

Gerry A greedy seller, three collectors and a couple of phone calls. You call that work?

Loren Who are you to judge . . .?

Gerry I lift people out of despair. I lift people out of depths. I help people who need helping. And it's hard and I bear the weight and it takes months, sometimes years, but hey, that's all boring, isn't it? Compared with the slick tongue and quick sell.

Loren St Gerry the backstabber.

Gerry Well, for Christ's sake. Hard work?

Loren All three dropped out at one stage or another. You have no idea what I've been through.

Gerry What have you been through?

Loren I'll tell you some day.

Gerry (*suspicious*) Tell me what?

Loren If I make a deal tonight, it'll be because I have to work out what's going on in people's heads too, but the difference is I have to do it instantly. OK, you've said your piece, now go! Bye.

Gerry Look, I don't necessarily want it to be over between us –

Loren Necessarily?

Gerry I just can't go through that again. I need a guarantee.

Loren Gerry, I'm not a kitchen appliance! Go!

Gerry looks at her and goes, slamming the door behind him. Loren slumps and talks to herself.

OK. Shake it off. Everything else out of your head. Focus. (*She breathes deeply.*) Breathe and focus. Breathe and focus. (*She takes a few more calming breaths, then dials.*)

SCENE TWO

Kel and Mindy's loft apartment. Intercut.
Mindy puts down a Pollock art book she's been staring at and picks up her mobile, which is playing 'The Ride of the Valkyries'. Kel watches in the background.

Mindy Hi.

Loren Mindy, it's Loren.

Mindy Loren, are you OK?

Loren I'm fine. Fine.

Mindy I was just a little worried that . . .

Loren What?

Mindy It was a bit heavy to put you in that, er, situation.

Loren I'm a big girl. I never do anything I don't want to do . . . Look, the bad news is you're not the highest offer. The good news is you're not far off. I mean if you want to stay in.

Mindy What's the high offer?

Loren Twenty million.

Mindy We're way off the pace.

Loren I know it seems a lot, but everyone who knows anything says that Jackson Pollock is the next Van Gogh.

Mindy (*nodding*) Jackson Pollock is the next Van Gogh.

Loren There's a feeding frenzy out there for Abstract Expressionism. Curators from all over the world are out hunting in packs like barracuda. (*to audience*) Do barracuda hunt in packs? I have no idea.

Mindy I'll talk to Kel.

Loren Sure. Call me back.

Mindy Twenty million's a lot.

Kel (*taking the phone*) Too much, Loren.

Loren Oh, hi, Kel.

Kel Too much.

Mindy (*taking the phone back*) I'll talk to Kel.

Loren Sure. Get back to me.

Mindy Loren, I've been thinking about you a lot. I just didn't want you to think that I just saw you as –

Loren Don't apologise. Call me later when you know what you wanna do.

She hangs up. Mindy frowns.

Mindy She's mad at me.

Kel So what?

Mindy I shouldn't've done that stuff with her. She feels used.

Kel Who's using who? What was that bullshit about the next Van Gogh?

Mindy Curates are hot for him. They're out hunting in packs like . . . some sort of fish.

Kel It's bullshit, Sugar Plum. There are dozens of painters dealers are calling the next Van Gogh. Check it out on the net.

Mindy frowns.

She's a liar, Mindy. Don't be so fucking naive.

Mindy Every salesman lies a bit when they're selling.

Kel We're *not* buying the painting, Buttercup.

Mindy I'm sick of you assuming you make all the decisions.

Kel We're *not* buying the painting. It's dated crap from an artist whose reputation is on the way down.

Mindy Will you take a *look* at the painting for once instead of just getting second-hand opinions off the net like you always do. Take a fucking *look*!

She shoves the art book under his nose. Kel looks, then looks away.

I'm sick of all this 'future' bullshit.

Kel We're future people. That's why we're rich.

Mindy The truth is we're just running a shop. The corner store, just bigger. Our life is boring, Kel. That – (*She points at the painting.*) – has magic. We know it's beautiful but we don't know why. And that's magic.

Kel Roses are beautiful and we don't know why, but they're not twenty million a bunch.

Mindy We didn't make the roses, Kel. But someone *made* that painting. And I think that's magic, and I want some of that sort of magic in my life.

Kel C'mon, you want Loren in your life.

Mindy Yeah, maybe I do. Maybe I do. Maybe I need some of that type of magic too. I'm sick of pretending *we've* still got a relationship.

Kel Pretending? Mindy, don't do this.

Mindy I'm sorry about your dick. But I told you not to do it and you chose to go right ahead.

Kel If you'd admitted you were gay –

Mindy I'm not 'gay'. I'm bi, like everyone else.

Kel – then I wouldn't have kept blaming our dead bed on my dick!

Mindy Kel, there's never been a woman in *creation* who comes every time. You're too greedy, Kel. You want to be number one at everything. It wasn't good enough that it was big, it had to be *huge*. Well, it is. It's just a little bit of a problem that the only thing you can make love to is your own belly button. I'm sorry, but you did it to yourself and I'm sick of feeling guilty! I want that painting.

Kel You want her.

Mindy I want a life that doesn't involve twenty hours a day taking perfume orders from the panic-stricken.

Kel What are you telling me? You're going to walk out on the business?

Mindy Yeah.

Kel I can't run the thing on my own.

Mindy Kel, I'm sick of dot com and I'm sick of our life.

Kel OK, we're an electronic corner store. So why is that so bad? A hell of a lot of people led very happy lives running corner stores. OK, they weren't painting great works, but they were providing a service that people need. And that's what we're doing. Letting people say, 'I'm sorry. I still love you.'

Mindy If they can remember what love means they're luckier than I am. I just do public sex acts for a fucked-up voyeur!

Kel looks stricken.

Sorry, sorry. I didn't mean to be that mean. Sorry. But that's what staying together is doing to me.

Kel Babe, we'll stop doing the coke. We'll stop the sex shit. If you walked out there'd be nothing left. We're the A-team.

Mindy Kel, honey. For both our sakes I've got to get out.

Kel (*hurt, angry*) Just tell me. Just tell me. Exactly *what* is this new spiritually fulfilling life you're aiming for?

53

Mindy I don't know! Just not what I'm doing now. (*Mindy picks up her mobile phone.*)

Kel You're not buying that overpriced piece of shit.

Mindy I'm going to do what I wanna do!

> *Mindy punches numbers into her mobile phone.*
> *Kel gets up, throws the art book away and walks out.*
> *Loren's apartment.*
> *Loren's phone plays 'Ballet des Champs-Élysées'.*
> *Loren grabs it.*
> *Mindy and Kel's apartment. Intercut.*
> *Mindy retrieves the art book and opens the page to the Pollock.*

Loren?

Loren Mindy.

Mindy It's a beautiful painting, and I want it. Just don't know about twenty million. Can you call me when you need an answer?

Loren I won't sell it without calling you first.

Mindy Thanks. And I am sorry.

Loren Mindy, listen, it *was* a little bizarre, but I let it happen.

Mindy I just don't want you to hate me.

Loren I don't hate you.

Mindy Thank you. (*She hangs up and stares through tear-filled eyes at the painting.*)

Loren (*to audience*) And I don't think I do. Or maybe I'm just trying to sell a painting. (*Loren dials.*)

SCENE THREE

Loren's apartment. Seconds later.
  Dawn's apartment. Intercut.
  Dawn, who is pouring herself a vodka, picks up her
apartment phone.

Dawn Dawn Grey.

Loren Dawn, it's Loren. You're not the top bidder, but
you're not far off.

  There's a silence.

Dawn, are you there?

Dawn Yes.

Loren The top offer is twenty. Are you there?

Dawn Yes.

Loren Do you want to think about it.

Dawn Yes.

Loren Could you ring me back? I'd like to tie this up
tonight.

Dawn I'll ring you back.

  She hangs up the phone. So does Loren, who is
  puzzled and perplexed at the total lack of response.
  Dawn sits there staring straight ahead. Loren dials
  another number. Manny and Phyllis are waiting.
  Manny picks up the phone.

SCENE FOUR

Manny's apartment. Intercut

Manny Yeah.

Loren Manny.

Manny Yeah.

Loren You're the top offer.

Manny I'm withdrawing it.

Loren You're what?

Phyllis You're what?

> *Manny puts his hand over the phone in a rage and turns on his wife.*

Manny Will you shut up. Will you please just shut up! If you want this painting let me handle it!

Phyllis This is one time in my life you're not going to bully me. I want that painting.

Manny *You'll get it!* Let me handle this please? Will you just please leave the room, or I'm going to hang up, I swear to God I'm going to hang up.

> *He waits until a glaring Phyllis retreats, then takes his hand off the phone.*

The bid is off.

Loren Manny, I humiliated myself for you.

Manny *You* humiliated yourself? How do you think I feel?

Loren Who gives a fuck what you feel?

Manny You were brilliant. Posing as my confidante, getting me to spill my guts, playing on my weaknesses. The bid's off.

Loren I've got it in writing.

Manny You've got zilch. This is not an official auction.

Loren You scumbag!

Manny I was desperate and you took advantage of me.

Loren It was the most degrading thing I've ever done.

Manny You know something? I think you liked it.

Loren You wish.

Manny I was so full of shame afterwards I wanted to die.

Loren That's such bullshit. You just want an excuse to welsh on a deal.

Manny (*angry*) The bid's seventeen point five. That's it.

Loren There's an eighteen point five offer on the table already.

Manny Bullshit!

Loren Then it goes to the other party.

Manny Eighteen point six – that's it. Get back to me.

He hangs up. Phyllis comes back into the room.

Phyllis So did we get it?

Manny No we didn't get it! (*He sits tensely by the phone.*)

Phyllis I want it, Manny.

Manny I *know* you want it. I know, I know, I know, I know – I'm trying to get it! Now will you just shut up? She's going to call back.

Loren and Gerry's apartment. Shortly after.
  Loren sits there waiting for Dawn to call. Gerry comes back in.

Loren What?

Gerry So how's it going?

Loren (*fighting to keep back her tears*) That piece of slime Manny Davis withdrew his offer as soon as he heard he was top bid.

Gerry Withdrew?

Loren Yeah!

Gerry Can he do that?

Loren He just did. I'm back to eighteen point six.

Gerry Jesus.

Loren Yeah. Almost a million and a half. My debt. Not yours.

Gerry A million and a half. Oh Jesus.

Loren It's not your problem!

Gerry How in hell are you ever going to clear yourself of that?

Loren The auction's not over yet.

Gerry Didn't I tell you this was crazy?

Loren Yes, you told me, now go!

Gerry Who's still bidding?

Loren All of them, Gerry. Get out of my space and let me think. Please.

Gerry This is a disaster. You'll never get them up to twenty.

Loren I've got leverage.

Gerry What?!

Loren Just a few phone calls. That's all you think it took to get this happening?

Gerry What kind of leverage?

Loren Go! Go away.

Gerry (*sudden insight*) You fucked Manny Davis, didn't you?

Loren No!

Gerry That's why he offered twenty million!

Loren He withdrew the offer.

Gerry Yes, because now he's pissed at how you got it. Right?

Loren Wrong!

Gerry Loren, I know guilt when I see it.

Loren Gerry, do you know what's going to happen if I fuck up here? I lose everything. I haven't got time to listen to your moralising.

Gerry (*moralistically*) I'm not being moralistic about the act itself. It's what the act reveals about your psyche. Manipulative behaviour like that is bordering on the sociopathic.

Loren Thank you, doctor. I've advanced from hysteric to sociopath and the evening's still young.

Gerry Please, Loren, please be honest. Have you or have you not had sex with any of the bidders?

Loren Yes, I had sex with one of the bidders, and it was more exciting than it's ever been with you!

Gerry stares at her in shock and goes.

(*to* audience) Oh my God. Extreme stress, that's all I can put it down to. And being called a sociopath. Which I'm starting to believe I am.

SCENE SIX

The three bidders sit in their respective apartments thinking as Loren waits.
Dawn's apartment.
Dawn pours herself a large vodka and tonic. It's not the first.

Dawn (*to* audience) Twenty million. Even eighteen point five was a stupid offer. At least half a million more than it was worth, but I just wanted to get this over and done with and honestly, my corporate clients couldn't care less. 'Just get it,' was the instruction.

Loren's apartment. Intercut.

Loren (*to* audience) Ethically I should call Dawn and tell her that the top offer is now only eighteen point six.

Dawn (*to* audience) Ever since I can remember, colour, line and form excited me more than anything. At school, my art teachers were always kind, but when I showed them my work a sort of . . . sadness would infuse their voices as they said, 'Dawn, that's really interesting.'
So after Bedales, I was off to St Martin's, but I learned nothing except that whatever it is that makes great art, I didn't have it. Well, if I couldn't do it myself, then the next best thing was to discover the secrets of those who

could. I had to know, to the point of total obsession, why some paintings were so moving, so profound and so deeply satisfying, and why others were not. So next, the Courtauld, where I read millions and millions of words, learned to parrot back the right opinions at the right time, and at twenty-six found myself with a PhD in fine arts. But art retained its secrets as it always will. I loved Cézanne, Picasso, Matisse, but all the words in the world were never going to explain why. (*She sighs.*) So if I couldn't make art, couldn't fathom art, what was left to do? Obvious – make money – squillions. Huge Manhattan apartment where I could walk to the best art in the world. But even that's proved scant compensation for the fact that I'm never going to create or say anything truly original in my life. (*A pause as her anger gathers.*) Fuck it! I'm going to make a stand. Against art as a commodity, art as a status game, art as just another speculative money-making trick in a world becoming greedy to the point of insanity. Twenty million is a crazy price and I'm not going to be part of this. And if my corporate clients decided to get rid of me, then so be it. Fuck 'em! Where's the bloody phone!

Before she can find it, it rings.

Dawn Dawn Grey.

Loren Dawn, it's Loren. I thought I should tell you that the top bidder has reduced his offer to eighteen point six.

Dawn Reduced? How can you reduce an offer you've already made?

Loren This particular client is probably the world's least trustworthy human being.

Dawn Manny Davis.

Loren You know Manny.

Dawn I worked as a consultant for his wife's collection. Briefly. (*to audience*) Until he started inviting me up to his hotel suite and started to hint at things that were *extremely* distasteful. Suddenly I have a motive for wanting the painting. Anything that could possibly make Manny miserable will make me feel *great*. And after all, it's not my money I'm spending. (*to Loren*) Nineteen.

Loren You're sure.

Dawn I'm sure.

Loren I'll get back to you.

Dawn Thank you.

Loren You had a bad experience with Manny?

Dawn I don't think I should comment. (*Puts the phone down.*)

Loren (*to audience*) Oh God, Dawn? Yikes! (*Loren dials her apartment phone.*)

SCENE SEVEN

Manny's apartment. Intercut.
  Manny answers.

Manny Yeah?

Loren Nineteen.

Manny You're bullshitting me.

Loren I'm not.

Manny I want the name of the person. I want to check.

Loren No, Manny. If you want to pull out that's your decision. There is an offer of nineteen.

Manny It's not worth that!

Loren That's the offer I've got.

Manny No one is going to offer nineteen.

Loren I don't have to put up with this. I'm telling you the truth. If you don't want to believe me, then go to hell.

Loren cuts the connection. Manny turns to Phyllis.

Manny It's over. Some prick has offered nineteen.

Phyllis Because it's worth it.

Manny No it's not.

Phyllis Someone else thinks it is.

Manny That's because they're a moron.

Phyllis Manny, you can't lose on a Pollock.

Manny I'm not paying that.

Phyllis Get on the phone. There have to be occasional compensations for the hell of living with you.

Manny Wait, wait – the hell of living with me? Excuse me, am I hearing right? Look around you. Some hell.

Phyllis Hell.

Manny There'd be a lot of women who wouldn't mind this sort of hell.

Phyllis Do you really think that money makes up for the rest of it?

Manny 'Rest' of it? What 'rest' are you talking about?

Phyllis You know . . .

Manny Huh?

Phyllis Little things like driving your son to the point of suicide.

Manny If you hadn't spoiled and pampered him from the day he was born he might've learned to stand on his own two feet.

Phyllis He is standing on his own two feet.

Manny Oh yeah, sure – in San Francisco. The fag capital of the world.

Phyllis There's something really sick about what you did to Nathan.

Manny Try and give him the skills he needed to succeed? That's sick?

Phyllis Stand by watching Matthew and Robert beat him up? That's not sick?

Manny My brothers beat the shit out of me, it was the best thing that ever happened, it made me vow that I'd trample on them one day. And believe me I have.

Phyllis You've got a primitive mind, Manny. You think if you end up richer than someone, you've somehow won. The only thing you've ever achieved in your whole life is make a huge number of people hate you.

Manny Respect me. Not hate. Respect.

Phyllis Manny, they hate you.

Manny You've been getting all this from Nathan, haven't you? Calling San Francisco three times a day.

Phyllis I'm not stupid, Manny. I don't need Nathan to tell me what people think of you.

Manny I'm tough, I don't take prisoners, I do the best deal I can do, and I never break the law. I'm just good. That's what they hate.

Phyllis Manny, any man that hates his son is a sad, sick human being.

Manny I don't hate my son. I hate the fact that he takes it up the ass.

Phyllis That's it, Manny. If you *ever* say that again, I'm walking.

Manny Go.

Phyllis I warn you, I will.

Manny Every connection you have in the world is because I'm your husband. Do you know that every invitation we get is because I'm your husband? Do you think they'd want you on their charity committees and Opera House boards if you were divorced? C'mon now, Phyllis, get real. Now do you want this 'Wow' painting or don't you?

Phyllis No, Manny, I don't.

Manny You don't?

Phyllis What's the point? When the only thrill in life is trying to make my friends sick with envy, then I'm in big trouble.

Manny Walk, go on, walk. See your divorce lawyer. Loot all you can get.

Phyllis Manny, what *is* there left?

Manny History. A lifetime together. That's what's left.

Phyllis History? Years and years of watching you hate our youngest boy.

Manny I don't hate Nathan! I just hate the fact he takes it – (*up the ass!*)

Phyllis I warned you, Manny!

Manny When he was little I loved him more than the other two. You know that.

Phyllis Until the day you suspected –

Manny Do *you* like the fact that he takes it –

Phyllis *Back off, Manny!* Right now or you'll *really* be sorry, and I'm not talking divorce, or money.

Manny Then what the hell *are* you talking about?

Phyllis Manny, we've had separate bedrooms for fifteen years now. I wonder why.

Manny Because I snore. That's why.

Phyllis Manny. Our marriage is a sham. I've hung on in there because being the wife of Manny Davis *has* opened a lot of doors. No matter how much they hate the man who made the money, they welcome with open arms the wife who might send some of it their way.

Manny How did we get here? I don't want to be here. I was buying you a painting. All I ever try and do is make you happy.

    He reaches for the phone.
        Loren's apartment. Intercut.
        Loren answers.

Loren Loren.

Manny Manny. Nineteen point five. That's it.

Loren Can I believe you this time?

Manny Nineteen point five.

Loren What – then you back out on me tomorrow?

Manny No, I won't.

Loren I'll call you back. (*She hangs up and looks thoughtful.*)

Phyllis I don't *want* you to buy me the painting.

Manny Let's not do this. You want the painting. It makes me feel good getting it for you. OK?

Phyllis I don't want it.

Manny Sweetheart, I want you to have the painting and I want you here with me. If you walked out it'd destroy me. You've picked me up when I've been rock-bottom. You've given me courage. You've given me strength. No man can achieve what I did without a wife like you, Phyllis.

Phyllis looks at him.

Phyllis I found a stack of your magazines ten years ago, Manny.

Manny What magazines?

Phyllis Men 'taking it up the ass' magazines.

Manny goes pale.

Who do you get to do it to you? Do you hire men?

Manny They were Nathan's magazines. Not mine.

Phyllis They were yours.

Manny No.

Phyllis Who does it to you, Manny?

Manny No one! No man has ever, *ever* done anything to me. And never will.

Phyllis You were never really interested in me, were you?

Manny Of course I was.

67

Phyllis I knew that if I wanted real passion I had to look elsewhere. I'm sorry, but I did.

Manny Who? Who?

Phyllis Men who wanted me.

Manny Who?!

Phyllis They're your children. Don't worry. They're all yours. Even Nathan. Who you've always had far more in common with than you want to admit. Right?

Manny That's not true.

Phyllis You both 'take it up the ass'. Right?

Manny Don't say that.

Phyllis Well don't you say it. About Nathan. *Ever again!* (*She gets up to go.*)

Manny Do you want the painting?

Phyllis *No!*

Manny But I've already made a bid, Phyllis.

Phyllis Then donate it to a gallery, because it's not coming inside this house!

She goes. Manny stares straight ahead, then picks up the phone, then puts it down. He stares straight ahead.

SCENE EIGHT

Loren's apartment.
  Loren picks up the phone and dials.
  Dawn's apartment. Intercut.
  Dawn answers.

Dawn Dawn Grey.

Loren Dawn. Look – I'm sorry. He's gone up to nineteen point five.

Dawn sits there thinking. The vodka and tonic she has been drinking all evening is finally having an effect.

Dawn Twenty!

Loren Dawn?

Dawn Twenty.

Loren Are you sure?

Dawn Absolutely sure. What could be better than to make Manny furious *and* waste corporate cash.

Loren Are you sure you're in a fit state?

Dawn Of course I'm not in a fit state. I'm pissed out of my fucking brains. But not so pissed that I won't remember in the morning. Twenty.

She laughs delightedly, puts the phone down and pours herself another large vodka and tonic and settles back in her chair chuckling.

Loren's apartment.
Loren hesitates, then gets on the phone.

Manny's apartment. Intercut.
Manny answers.

Loren Manny, the offer is twenty.

Manny They can have it.

Loren You're sure?

Manny I've never been surer of anything in my life. (*He hangs up. He picks up the phone again, then puts it down and continues to stare straight ahead.*)

Loren's apartment.

Loren (*to audience*) Twenty million. Not a cent for myself, but I break even.

> *Mindy's apartment. Intercut.*
> *Mindy, who has been staring at the reproduction of the Pollock since we last left her, picks up her mobile and dials. Loren's mobile plays the first bars of Beethoven's Fifth. Loren answers.*

Loren Hi, Mindy.

Mindy Hi.

Loren It's still twenty.

Mindy It's a wonderful painting.

Loren It is.

Mindy Kel and I are finished.

Loren Really?

Mindy If I buy it, it's me buying. He's out.

Loren I'm sorry to hear that. About you and Kel.

> *Mindy has tears in her eyes.*

Mindy Loren, I wanted you, but I didn't want you with him watching.

Loren Mindy –

Mindy It's the truth.

Loren Mindy –

Mindy Did you feel anything?

Loren Yes . . . But . . . Yes.

Mindy I'm buying the painting. I don't care how much it costs.

Loren Mindy, if you're –

Mindy It's my declaration of love. You can take it or leave it, no strings attached.

Loren Look, buy this painting if you want it. That's the only reason you should buy it. If you want it.

Mindy I want it. Whatever it costs. OK, so I'm not thinking straight. I don't care. I'm totally hooked. The only thing that's going to stop me buying that painting is if you tell me you don't feel just a little bit of what I feel for you.

Loren Yeah . . . well, kind of.

Mindy I knew it.

Loren But that doesn't mean –

Mindy Loren, it's not just the physical thing. It's a life together. I can see it. And on our wall will be the Jackson Pollock. And we'll know why it's there.

Loren Mindy –

Mindy You feel something too. I know you do. You admitted it.

Loren Oh dear.

Mindy Suddenly I know what life's all about. Twenty-one, twenty-two, I don't care what I pay.

Loren (*to audience*) Twenty-two means two for me. Two fucking million! Ninety-nine per cent of me is screaming, 'Do it, for fuck's sake, do it.' (*to Mindy*) Mindy . . .

Mindy OK, you're not as blown away by me as I am by you, but we'll get there. I know it. I just know it.

Loren Mindy –

Mindy We'll get there.

Loren Whatever you pay for it, all you'll get is the painting.

Mindy Don't say that.

Loren I have to say it. I like you, but you and I and the painting on the wall isn't going to be where I end up.

Mindy Can we try?

Loren Look, I hardly know you and it's not worth twenty-two million.

Mindy You care, I can hear it in your voice.

Loren Mindy, I care enough not to want you hating me five years down the line.

Mindy You care. I know you do.

Loren Mindy, I care. But I don't love you and I can't do this. OK? I can't do it!

There's a pause.

Mindy Can we meet this week? For coffee?

Loren OK. Get some sleep.

Mindy OK. Thank you. Goodnight. (*Mindy hangs up and sits there staring at the painting.*)

SCENE NINE

Loren's apartment. Shortly after.
Loren sits staring at the phone and punches in a number.
Dawn's apartment. Intercut.
Dawn, who is by now quite drunk, answers.

Dawn Dawn Grey.

Loren Dawn, it's yours.

Dawn What? The wimp gave in?

Loren My client declined to go higher.

Dawn Your client. Let me tell you something about your bloody client!

Loren Dawn, there's nothing you can tell me I don't already know.

There's a silence.

Dawn Twenty-one.

Loren Dawn? It's yours already.

Dawn You've earned it.

Loren Twenty-one?

Dawn What the bloody hell? It's being bought by a soulless corporation who wouldn't know art from their – collective assholes.

Loren raises her eyebrows.

Loren You're sure?

Dawn Twenty-two.

Loren Dawn, I feel uneasy about this.

Dawn Twenty-two.

Loren You're sure you haven't been drinking a little too much?

Dawn I'm sure I've been drinking far, far too much.

Loren No, no – You'll feel differently in the morning.

Dawn Twenty-three. Let the bastards pay!

Loren Dawn – Twenty-three . . . Are you serious?

73

Dawn sinks into her chair and lets out a sigh.

Dawn No, no, no. You're right, twenty. I'd never work again. It just would have been so wonderful to go to bed knowing I'd screwed them for three fucking million.

Loren I guess I could accept twenty-one.

Dawn Loren, I would love them to pay fifty million, but you're right. When I wake up in the morning I'd hate myself for being 'unprofessional'. I can't stand myself when I'm sober.

Loren I could accept twenty point five.

Dawn No. In the grey, grey dawn, it would dawn on Dawn Grey that alcohol had taken her senses away. Yes, yes, yes. My client's final offer is twenty million dollars. (*She raps an imaginary hammer down.*) Sold, to the gutless stooge of corporate thugs for two million more than it's worth. We must have a drink one day.

Loren Yeah, sure. (*to audience*) I doubt I could keep up.

SCENE TEN

Loren's apartment. Shortly after.
  Gerry comes in the door.

Gerry Well?

  Loren looks at him.

Gerry The debt. How much?

Loren What do you care?

Gerry Of course I care.

Loren About me? Tell me. What's the name of that little brown creature that deserts sinking ships?

Gerry Loren –

Loren It's slipped my memory. Is it a hamster? A gerbil?

Gerry Loren, you did something that was insanely risky and expected me to pick up the tab?

Loren Oh, I remember. It's a *rat*!

Gerry Loren do you really think what you did was *fair*?!

Loren No! I should have sat down and talked about it for a month. Problem was I had an hour to decide and *you weren't there.*

Gerry Do you really think it was fair?!

Loren No, Gerry, it wasn't fair. And you went to your lawyer and he made you feel good about the fact that *you* weren't being fair. So what! You won't be footing the bill, will you? It's my problem.

Gerry And on top of that you screw your clients and tell me it's much more exciting with them than it's *ever* been with me!

Loren I was angry!

Gerry Did he or didn't he?!

Loren Did who?

Gerry Manny? Fuck you?

Loren I swear by all forty-seven Hindu gods, Manny did not fuck *me*.

Gerry *Something* happened between you.

Loren Do we have to do this?

Gerry If our marriage has any future –

Loren You've made it very clear that it doesn't.

Gerry If we have any future I have to know.

Loren I don't want to do this, Gerry.

Gerry I have to know!

She looks at him. Deliberating. Then makes a decision Then decides that if he's that desperate to know, she'll tell him.

Loren He didn't fuck me. I fucked him. With a very large dildo. He seemed to enjoy it a lot. It's something you should think about if you ever have a gap in your life.

Gerry Is there *anything* you wouldn't do?

Loren Let me think. Apparently not. I also had sex with Mindy while Kel watched.

Gerry Oh my God!

Loren And I enjoyed it. So don't feel the least bit guilty about dumping me. I'm a stretched-canvas whore.

Gerry You enjoyed it? While Kel watched? So what does that mean for us?

Loren You're the fucking psychologist!

Gerry You are one sick puppy.

Loren Whatever. Guilty as charged. Go and find yourself a lobotomised fuck-doll who thinks you're God.

Gerry I came back here because I was worried sick about you. I was going to say, 'Honey, your debt is our debt.' I was going to say, 'I don't care who you've screwed, I'm crazy about you and if we have to take out a huge loan and live in a goddam tent we'll see this through.' Well, forget all that. I've finally seen all the layers peeled off the onion of your psyche and what's underneath is *ugly*.

Loren You've diagnosed me already. Sociopath, right?

Gerry Straight out of the textbooks.

Loren Hysteric?

Gerry Queen of all drama queens.

Loren Borderline personality?

Gerry At your core there's nothing but a gaping void.

Loren Is there any personality disorder I *don't* have?

Gerry Yeah! Depressive. Like I said, they're honest.

Loren Glad you've got that off your chest?

Gerry Extremely.

Loren I'll pack my stuff and go.

Gerry How much did you lose?

Loren Does it matter?

She walks out. He watches her go. He frowns.

SCENE ELEVEN

Manny's house. Late at night
   Manny is still sitting by the phone. He picks it up and this time dials.

Manny Nathan? Nathan! It's your father. Don't hang up. Please. No, no, your mother's fine. Listen. I've got something to say. Please, please, don't hang up. (*Pause.*) I'm flying to San Francisco tomorrow – (*Pause.*) No, not on business. To see *you*. To sit down and talk to you. Just half an hour. That's all I'm asking. (*Pause.*) OK, no, I understand you don't *think* there's anything from me you want to hear, but – Nathan, believe me, Nathan,

Nathan – (*Manny stares at the dead phone. He puts it back in the cradle. Tears form in his eyes. To himself*) You don't want to hear me admit that I've been a bastard and it's a wonder you're still sane? You don't want to hear that for the first time since you were a kid I want to put my arms around you and say I'm sorry. (*Manny picks up the phone and punches in numbers. Into phone*) Yeah, I want a direct flight to San Franciso in the morning. (*Pause.*) The earlier the better. (*Pause.*) Why is it every time I ring this airline the computer is 'down'. The truth is your computer is 'down' *every* day. And the reason is you're undercapitalised and your infrastructure is appalling. Stop making excuses and get me a fucking ticket!

SCENE TWELVE

Central Park. New York.

Loren (*to audience*) Slamming the door felt great for the first day or two, then the tears started. And when I wasn't crying I was walking down the middle of streets after midnight, ranting like a madwoman. (*She imitates herself ranting like a madwoman.*) 'I'm going to make it, Gerry, you asshole. The biggest collectors in town will be begging me to advise them. I'm going to be the High Priestess of art, the Guru. Everywhere I go, heads will turn. I'm going to be rich. Mega rich. So rich I'll be able to buy *twenty*, no *fifty* apartments like yours! But who'd want them? I'll have *mansions*. All over the world. I'll shuttle between them in my own private jet. I'll have butlers and assistants and my own private hairdresser. You wait, Gerry, you wait and see. I will have a lifestyle the whole fucking world will envy. And you'll wish you had've believed in me.'

78

But do I *really* want to sell my soul? Again . . . And again and again.

The woman I thought I wanted to be had come slamming into the woman I was. But just who the fuck was I?

Someone I don't like.

I rang Gerry last night. Had it all rehearsed. 'Forgive me. Let's try and work through all this shit. The best moments I've had in life were with you and I want them again. I want the kids we both wanted to have. I want the view we used to share.' I got three words out and he hung up.

So. Here I am. No money. No job. No husband.

But maybe it's a blessing. At least the greed dreams are over. And he might call back. If he doesn't, I'll start again.